PAPER CRAFTS FOR THE 4TH OF JULY

Randel McGee

LIBERTY

Enslow Elementary

an imprint of

Enslow Publishers, Inc.

40 Industrial Road
Box 398
Berkeley Heights, NJ 07922
USA

http://www.enslow.com

This book meets the National Standards for Arts Education.

Enslow Elementary, an imprint of Enslow Publishers, Inc.
Enslow Elementary® is a registered trademark of Enslow Publishers, Inc.

Library of Congress Cataloging-in-Publication Data

McGee, Randel.
    Paper crafts for the 4th of July / Randel McGee.
       p. cm. — (Paper craft fun for holidays)
    Includes bibliographical references and index.
    Summary: "Explains the significance of Independence Day and how to make 4th-of-July-themed crafts
       out of paper"— Provided by publisher.
    ISBN 978-0-7660-3727-4
    1. Fourth of July decorations—Juvenile literature. 2. Paper work—Juvenile literature. I. Title.
    TT900.F68M33 2012
    745.594'1—dc22
                2010038621

Paperback ISBN: 978-1-59845-332-4

Printed in the United States of America

052011 Lake Book Manufacturing, Inc., Melrose Park, IL

10 9 8 7 6 5 4 3 2 1

To Our Readers: We have done our best to make sure all Internet Addresses in this book were active and appropriate when we went to press. However, the author and the publisher have no control over and assume no liability for the material available on those Internet sites or on other Web sites they may link to. Any comments or suggestions can be sent by e-mail to comments@enslow.com or to the address on the back cover.

Every effort has been made to locate all copyright holders of material used in this book. If any errors or omissions have occurred, corrections will be made in future editions of this book.

♻ Enslow Publishers, Inc., is committed to printing our books on recycled paper. The paper in every book contains 10% to 30% post-consumer waste (PCW). The cover board on the outside of each book contains 100% PCW. Our goal is to do our part to help young people and the environment too!

Illustration Credits: Crafts prepared by Randel McGee; photography by Nicole diMella/Enslow Publishers, Inc.; Shutterstock, pp. 5, 19, 26.

Cover Illustration: Crafts prepared by Randel McGee; photography by Nicole diMella/Enslow Publishers, Inc.

Contents

AUTHOR'S NOTE: Many of the materials used in making these crafts may be found by using recycled paper products. The author uses such recycled items as cereal boxes and similar packaging for light cardboard, used manila folders for card stock paper, leftover pieces of wrapping paper, and so forth. This not only reduces the cost of the projects but is also a great way to reuse and recycle paper. Be sure to ask an adult for permission before using any recycled paper products.

The projects in this book were created for this particular holiday. However, I invite readers to be imaginative and find new ways to use the ideas in this book to create different projects of their own. Please feel free to share pictures of your work with me through www.mcgeeproductions.com. Happy Crafting!

INDEPENDENCE DAY!

In Philadelphia, Pennsylvania, in early July 1776, a group of men from each of the thirteen American colonies gathered to discuss a problem. The group was called the Second Continental Congress, and they wanted to solve the colonies' problems with the British government, which controlled the colonies from far away in London, England. The king of England, George III, would not let the colonists have much to say in making decisions for their own people. When the American colonists protested, King George III sent British armies to America to force them to obey him. The colonists became very upset with this harsh, unfair treatment from their king. The Congress decided to declare that the American colonies were a free country and no longer under British rule. It was a bold and dangerous move.

Thomas Jefferson, from Virginia, was a member of the Second Continental Congress. He was asked to write an official document that would announce the Congress's decision to King George III. It is called the Declaration of Independence. It contains the famous lines: "We hold these truths to be self-evident, that all men are created equal, that they are endowed by their Creator with certain unalienable Rights, that among these are Life, Liberty and the pursuit of Happiness." These words have become famous around the world. At the end of the letter to the king, Jefferson wrote: "We, therefore . . . do solemnly publish and declare, That these united Colonies are, and of Right ought to be Free and Independent States." (Punctuation and capitalizations are from the original document.)

With these words, the Continental Congress declared that the American colonies were no longer British colonies, but a new, independent country. The Revolutionary War followed as England tried to win back control, but the Americans and their allies overcame the British forces and secured their right to govern themselves.

The Declaration of Independence was first signed on July 4, 1776, so that day became known as Independence Day. Independence Day, often called the "Fourth of July," was officially declared a national holiday by the Congress of the United States in 1870. It is considered the United States of America's birthday, and so the day is like a big party. It is celebrated with parades, speeches, and special programs with a patriotic theme. Families often enjoy the day with outdoor activities, picnics, and barbecues. Fireworks displays sponsored by the community light up the night skies, and many families have their own small fireworks displays. Red, white, and blue and the stars and stripes of the American flag appear everywhere on decorations and clothes. Show your American spirit with the crafts in this book!

American Flag Pennant

Since 1776, the United States of America has had a flag with a blue field decorated with white stars representing the states. The rest of the flag has alternating red and white stripes. A pennant is a long, slender flag, usually triangle-shaped, that is used for signaling others and for decoration. Make one or several as decorations for your Fourth of July celebration.

What you will need

- blue tissue paper or plastic table cover
- tracing paper
- pencil
- scissors
- white computer paper
- crepe paper streamers— red and white
- clear tape
- white glue
- yarn or string

WHAT TO DO

1. Fold the blue tissue paper or plastic table cover in half.

2. Use tracing paper and a pencil to trace the triangle pattern from page 40 onto the blue tissue paper or plastic table cover. Put the short side of the pattern on the fold. Cut out a triangle.

3. Transfer the star pattern to the white computer paper. Make two stars.

4. Cut the crepe paper streamers into 6-inch lengths. Make three red and two white.

5. Open up the triangle and tape or glue the paper streamers to one of the pointed ends. Alternate the colors: red, white, red, white, red. Let dry.

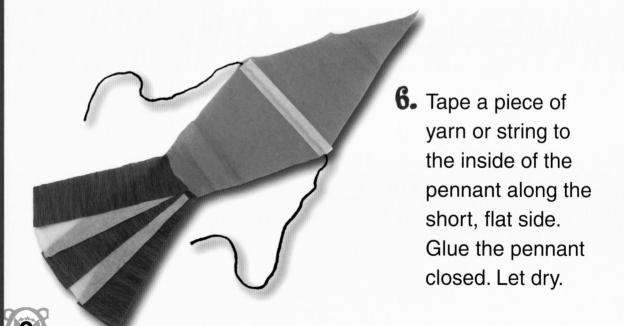

6. Tape a piece of yarn or string to the inside of the pennant along the short, flat side. Glue the pennant closed. Let dry.

7. Glue a white paper star on both sides of the pennant. Let dry.

8. Have an adult help you hang it as a decoration. You may want to put many pennants on a long string and hang them.

Paper Firework Fountain

Fireworks were first developed by the Chinese. They used small, bright explosives to celebrate special times and to symbolically drive away evil spirits. Today, fireworks are used around the world for special holidays and at happy events, such as Independence Day. This paper firework fountain looks like those you may see in your neighborhood.

What you will need

- white card stock
- tracing paper
- pencil
- tissue paper—assorted colors
- crayons or markers

- scissors
- silver pipe cleaners—9 to 12 pieces
- clear tape
- white glue
- construction paper—any color

WHAT TO DO

1. Transfer the cone pattern on page 41 to white card stock. Transfer the "flash" pattern from page 41 to tissue paper. Using tracing paper and a pencil may be helpful in copying the pattern.

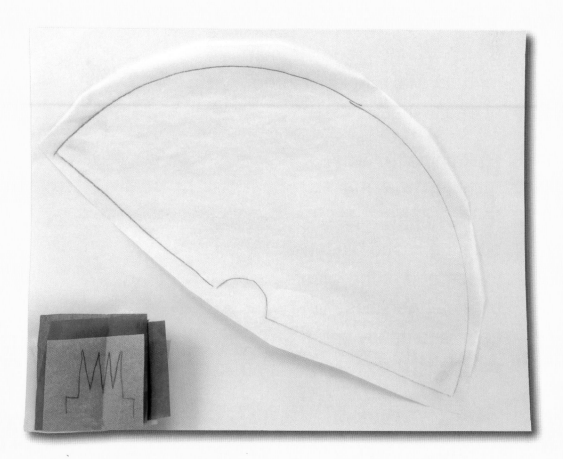

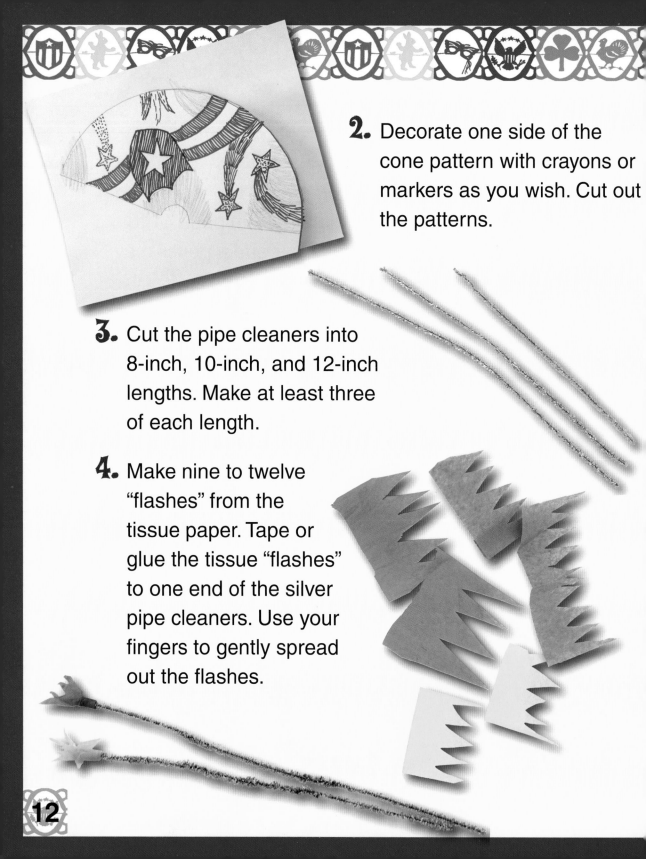

2. Decorate one side of the cone pattern with crayons or markers as you wish. Cut out the patterns.

3. Cut the pipe cleaners into 8-inch, 10-inch, and 12-inch lengths. Make at least three of each length.

4. Make nine to twelve "flashes" from the tissue paper. Tape or glue the tissue "flashes" to one end of the silver pipe cleaners. Use your fingers to gently spread out the flashes.

5. Tape or glue some "flashes" so that they stick out from the small half-circle on the flat side of the pattern. Tape nine or ten silver pipe cleaners to the inside of the cone so that they also stick out from the small half-circle.

6. Use tape to fasten the sides of the pattern together to form a cone.

7. Tape the bottom of the cone to a construction-paper base. Decorate the base as you wish.

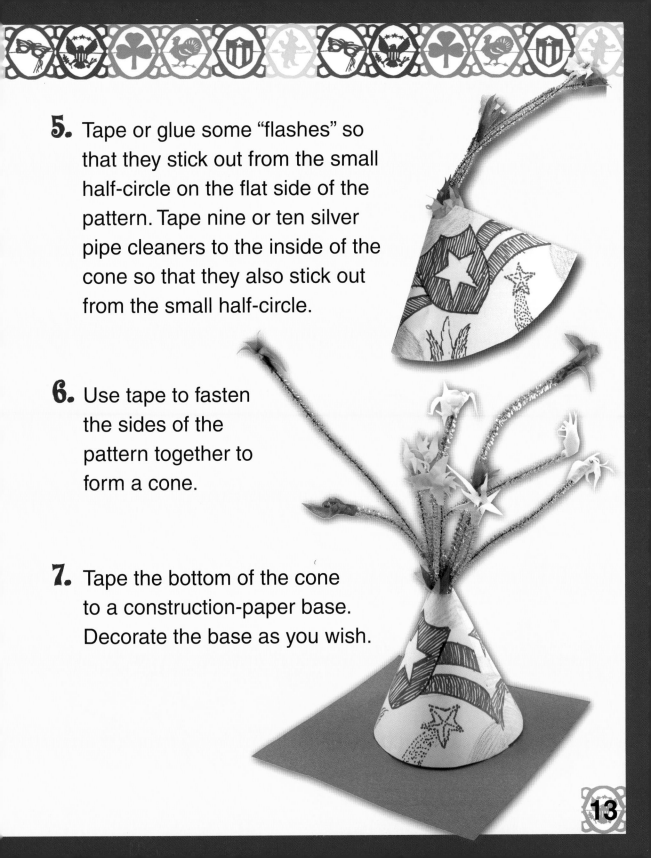

"The Bombs Bursting in Air"

"The bombs bursting in air" is a line from "The Star-Spangled Banner," the national anthem of the United States. It was written by Francis Scott Key during a cannon attack on an American fort by British warships on September 14, 1814, during the War of 1812. This decoration is a fire-free firework!

What You Will Need

- tracing paper
- pencil
- dark blue construction paper
- scissors
- star stickers
- metallic confetti (optional)
- clear tape
- gold or silver pipe cleaners
- white glue
- self-drying clay
- cardboard
- yellow tissue paper

WHAT TO DO

1. Transfer the burst patterns from page 39 to the blue construction paper. Tracing paper and a pencil may be useful in transferring the patterns.

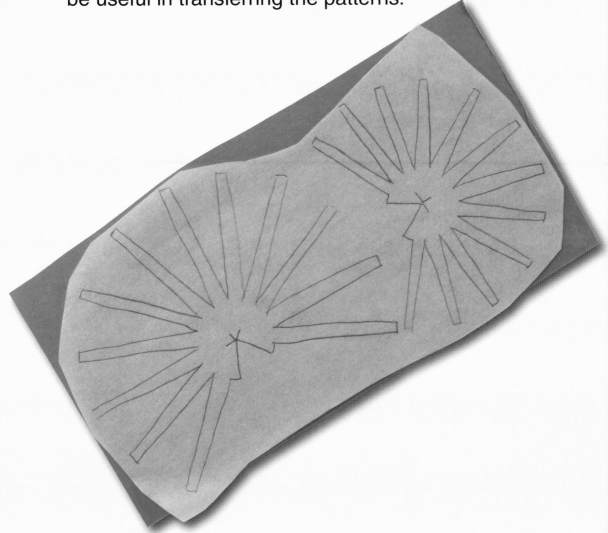

2. Cut out the patterns. Be sure to cut all the black lines of the pattern, including the little lines at the bottom of the burst.

3. Stick the star stickers on the end of each ray of the bursts and then at other places along the rays. Glue metallic confetti to the rays if you wish.

4. Carefully tape the bottom sides of the bursts together to form cone shapes of different sizes. The stars should face in.

5. Twist two pipe cleaners together. Curl one end of the doubled pipe cleaner into a tight little loop. Thread the plain end of the pipe cleaner through the center of the bursts in size order, smallest first. Use a drop of glue to secure each burst in place on the pipe cleaner. Let dry.

6. Take a walnut-sized piece of the self-drying clay and shape it into a small cone. Stick the plain end of the pipe cleaner into the top of the cone and push it down deep. Make sure it is secure. Put two or three pipe cleaners with the bursts into the clay and let the clay dry.

7. Use your fingers to curl the rays outward slightly.

8. Glue the bottom of the clay cone to a piece of colored cardboard as a base. Decorate the cone with yellow tissue paper strips to look like fire.

LIBERTY CROWN

The Statue of Liberty was a gift from France and was dedicated October 28, 1886. French sculptor Frederic Auguste Bartholdi designed it. Lady Liberty holds up the torch of freedom for the world to see. The seven rays on her crown stand for the seven continents of the world. It is made of copper and has a greenish gray color from being exposed to the weather.

WHAT YOU WILL NEED

- ✎ white poster board
- ✎ tracing paper
- ✎ pencil
- ✎ scissors
- ✎ crayons or markers
- ✎ clear tape

WHAT TO DO

1. Make a rectangle of poster board 7 x 14 inches. Fold it in half so that the short ends meet.

2. Use the tracing paper and a pencil to transfer the pattern from page 38 to the folded poster board. Be sure to place the dotted line of the pattern on the fold of the poster board.

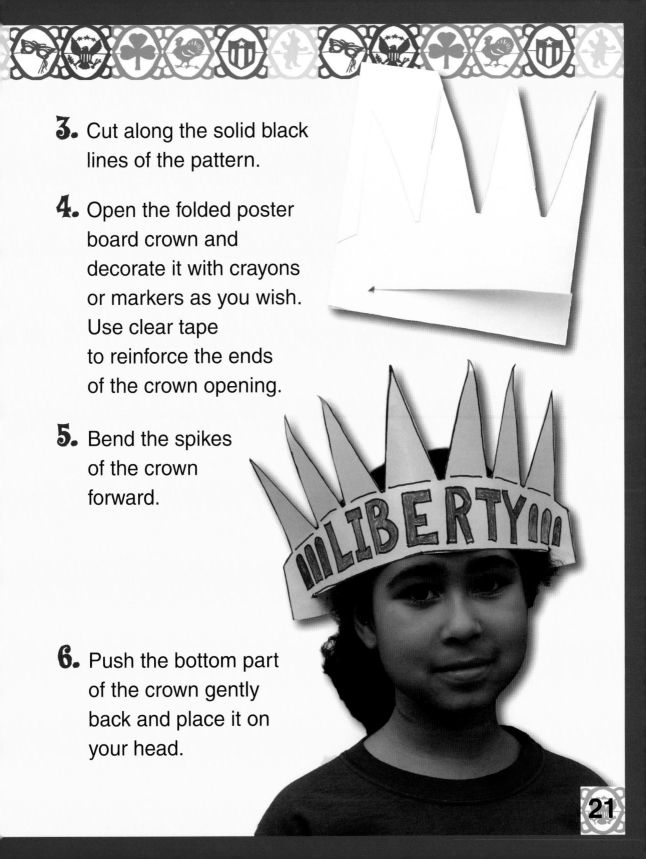

3. Cut along the solid black lines of the pattern.

4. Open the folded poster board crown and decorate it with crayons or markers as you wish. Use clear tape to reinforce the ends of the crown opening.

5. Bend the spikes of the crown forward.

6. Push the bottom part of the crown gently back and place it on your head.

LIBERTY

STARS AND STRIPES PAPER CHAIN

The flag of the United States of America is made up of stars and stripes and the colors red (for bravery), white (for purity), and blue (for justice). There is a star on the flag for each American state. The thirteen stripes represent the original thirteen colonies that became the United States. "The Stars and Stripes" is another name for the flag. Here are some stars and stripes to decorate for your Independence Day celebration!

WHAT YOU WILL NEED

- ✎ **tracing paper**
- ✎ **pencil**
- ✎ **construction paper— any colors**
- ✎ **scissors**

WHAT TO DO

1. Use the tracing paper and pencil to transfer the patterns from page 42 to the different colors of construction paper. You decide what color stars and stripes you want.

2. Cut out at least seven stripes
and six stars.

3. Fold in the sides of the arrow point of the
star pattern and slip the point through
the slot of the stripe pattern piece.

4. Open the folded points so that the arrow holds the pattern in place.

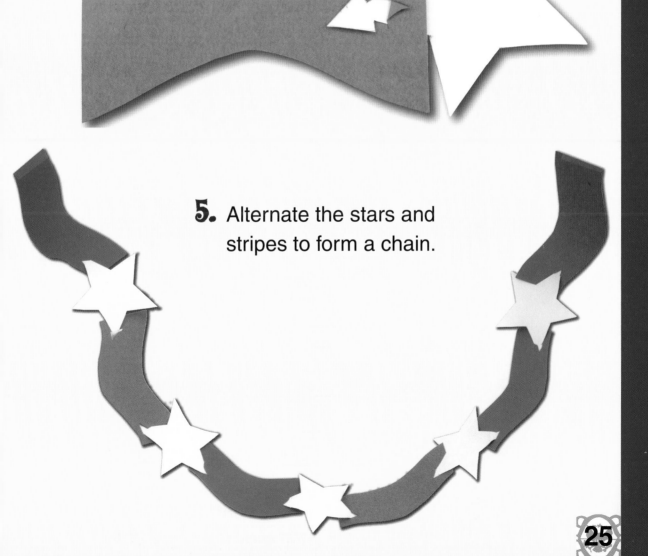

5. Alternate the stars and stripes to form a chain.

America's Uncle Sam

Uncle Sam is a pretend character who symbolizes the U.S.A. and its government. Legends say that barrels of meat sent to soldiers during the War of 1812 had the letters "U.S." stamped on the side. The soldiers joked that the meat came from their Uncle Sam.

What you will need

- ✎ **white card stock**
- ✎ **tracing paper**
- ✎ **pencil**
- ✎ **scissors**
- ✎ **colored pencils, crayons, or markers**
- ✎ **clear tape or white glue**

WHAT TO DO

1. Fold the card stock in half lengthwise.

2. Transfer the pattern from page 43 to the white card stock. Using tracing paper and a pencil may be helpful.

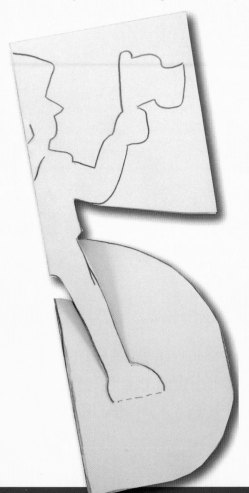

3. Cut out the pattern along the black lines.

4. Decorate the figure with colored pencils, crayons, or markers as you wish.

5. Fold the figure forward at the dashed lines on the bottom of the feet. Fold the arms, nose, and beard slightly as you wish.

6. Overlap points A and B as shown, and tape or glue the overlapping parts together behind the figure. Tape or glue points C and D to the base. Let dry, if needed.

7. Stand the figure up on a table to guide your Independence Day celebration.

An American Spectacle

A spectacle means a wonderful thing to see. It can also be something that helps you see wonderfully! You can show American spirit and watch an American show with spirit while wearing this patriotic eyewear!

What You Will Need

- poster board in any color—4 x 14 inches

- tracing paper

- pencil

- scissors

- crayons or markers

- glitter glue

- construction paper— any color (optional)

- white glue (optional)

- stickers (optional)

- clear tape (optional)

- blue or green cellophane (optional)

WHAT TO DO

1. Fold the poster board in half width-wise, so that the short sides meet.

2. Use tracing paper to transfer the spectacle pattern from page 41 to the poster board.

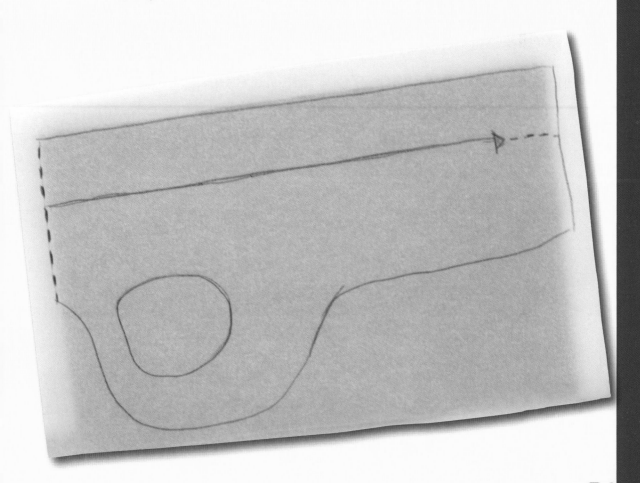

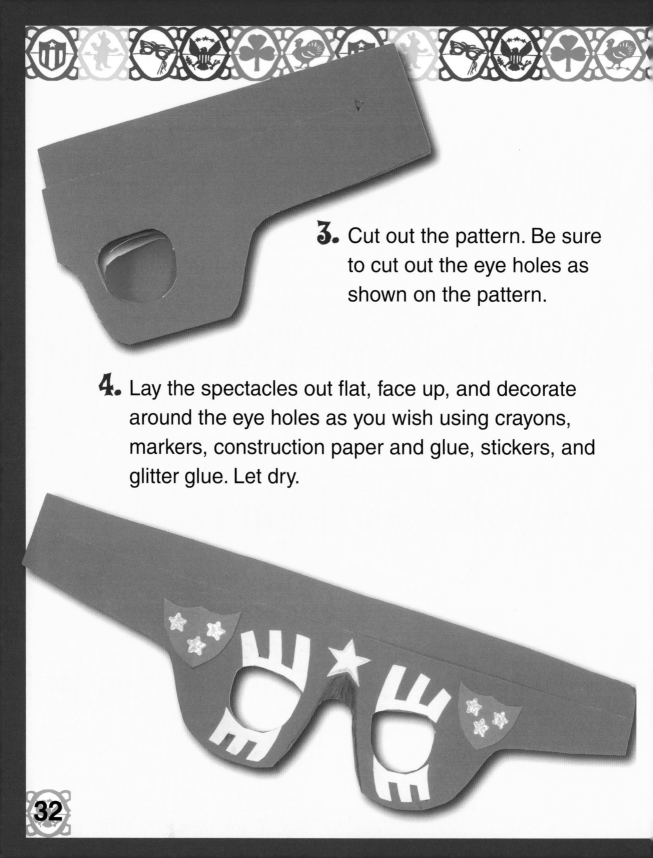

3. Cut out the pattern. Be sure to cut out the eye holes as shown on the pattern.

4. Lay the spectacles out flat, face up, and decorate around the eye holes as you wish using crayons, markers, construction paper and glue, stickers, and glitter glue. Let dry.

5. On the back side of the spectacles, tape some colored cellophane over the eye holes, if you wish.

6. Fold the poster board pattern along the dotted fold lines on the ends to form the head strap. Use a drop of white glue to hold the ends together. Let dry.

7. Gently push back the back strap, and slip the spectacles over your head.

"We the People" Patriotic Place Mats

What You Will Need

- tracing paper
- pencil
- scissors
- tan or light brown paper—12 x 18 inches (construction paper, butcher paper, or newsprint)
- crayons or makers

The Preamble of the Constitution states who wrote the Constitution and for whom: "We, the People of the United States . . ." This place mat can be a great reminder of the freedoms that we, the people of the United States, enjoy.

WHAT TO DO

1. Transfer the writing from page 42 to the top left corner of the tan or light brown paper (construction, butcher, or newsprint). Tracing paper and pencil may be helpful.

2. Use crayons or markers to trace around and fill in the writing on the light brown paper.

3. Decorate the place mat with other words that represent American standards, such as Liberty, Justice, Pursuit of Happiness, Rights, Freedom, Equality, and so on.

4. If you wish, rough up the edges of the place mat to make it look old and worn.

PATTERNS

The percentages included on the patterns tell you how much to enlarge or shrink the image using a copier. Most copiers and printers have an adjustable size/percentage feature to change the size of an image when you print it. After you print the patterns to their true sizes, cut them out or use tracing paper to copy them. Ask an adult to help you trace and cut the shapes.

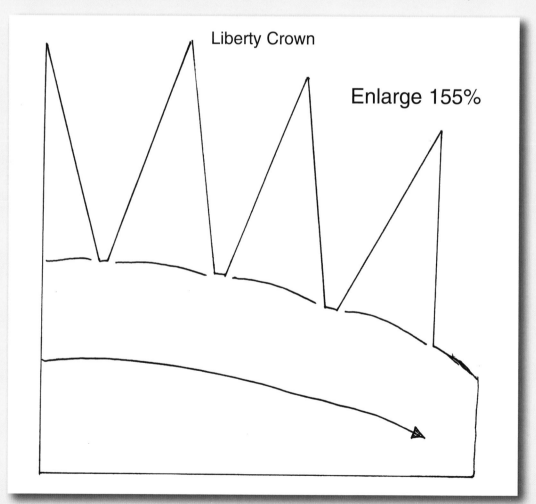

Liberty Crown

Enlarge 155%

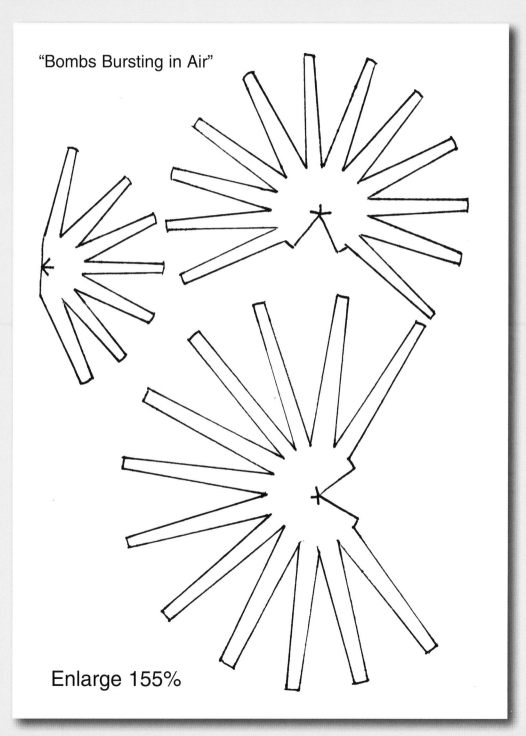

"Bombs Bursting in Air"

Enlarge 155%

American Flag Pennant

Enlarge 155%

An American Spectacle

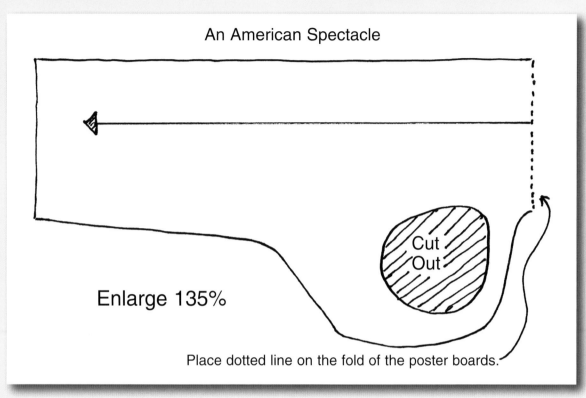

Enlarge 135%

Cut
Out

Place dotted line on the fold of the poster boards.

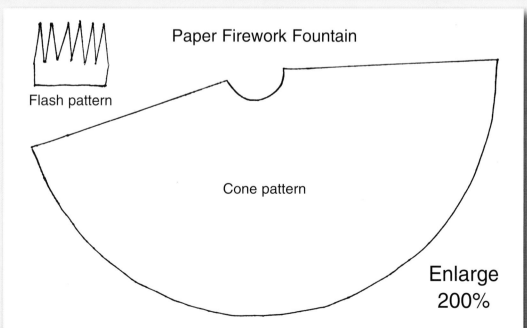

Paper Firework Fountain

Flash pattern

Cone pattern

Enlarge
200%

Patriotic Place Mats

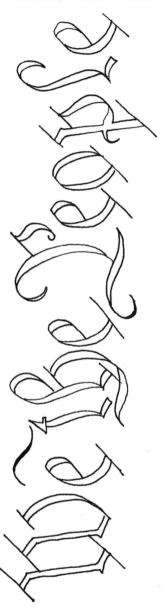

Enlarge 155%

Stars and Stripes Paper Chain

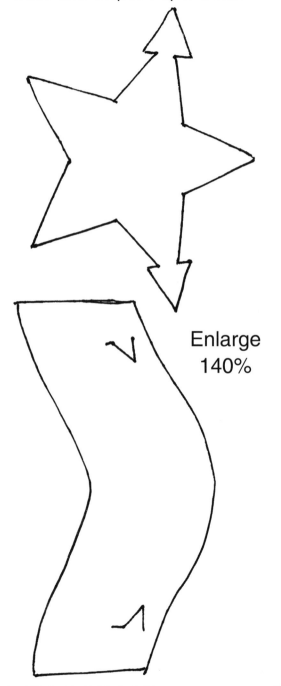

Enlarge
140%

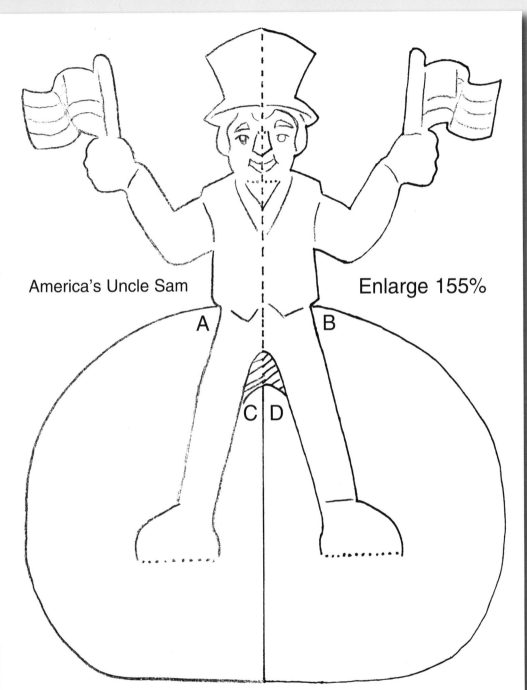

America's Uncle Sam

Enlarge 155%

A

B

C D

READ ABOUT

Books

Amato, Carol, and Ann D. Koffsky. *The Fourth of July: An Independence Day Feast of Fun, Facts, and Activities.* Hauppauge, N.Y.: Barron's, 2007.

Ansary, Mir Tamim. *Independence Day.* Chicago: Heinemann Library, 2006.

Heiligman, Deborah. *Celebrate Independence Day.* Washington, D.C.: National Geographic, 2007.

Internet Addresses

Kaboose: 4th of July/Independence Day Crafts
<http://crafts.kaboose.com/holidays/july-4/>

KinderArt: Independence Day Fourth of July Arts, Crafts, Lessons, and Activities
<http://www.kinderart.com/seasons/independenceday.shtml>

DLTK's: United States Crafts
<http://www.dltk-kids.com/usa/crafts.html>

Visit Randel McGee's Web site at
<http://www.mcgeeproductions.com>

Index

About the Author

Randel McGee has been playing with paper and scissors for as long as he can remember. As soon as he was able to get a library card, he would go to the library and find the books that showed paper crafts, check them out, take them home, and try almost every craft in the book. He still checks out books on paper crafts at the library, but he also buys books to add to his own library and researches paper-craft sites on the Internet.

McGee says, "I begin by making copies of simple crafts or designs I see in books. Once I get the idea of how something is made, I begin to make changes to make the designs more personal. After a lot of trial and error, I find ways to do something new and different that is all my own. That's when the fun begins!"

McGee has also liked singing and acting from a young age. He graduated from college with a degree in children's theater and specialized in puppetry. After college, he taught himself ventriloquism and started performing at libraries and schools with a friendly dragon puppet named Groark. "Randel McGee and Groark" have toured throughout the

United States and Asia, sharing their fun shows with young and old alike. Groark is the star of two award-winning video series for elementary school students on character education: *Getting Along With Groark* and *The Six Pillars of Character.*

In the 1990s, McGee combined his love of making things with paper with his love of telling stories. He tells stories while making pictures cut from paper to illustrate the tales he tells. The famous author Hans

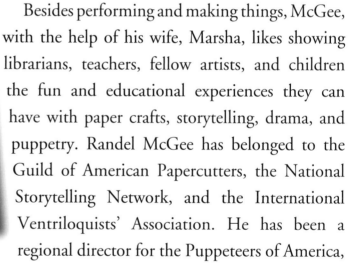

Christian Andersen also made cut-paper pictures when he told stories. McGee portrays Andersen in storytelling performances around the world.

Besides performing and making things, McGee, with the help of his wife, Marsha, likes showing librarians, teachers, fellow artists, and children the fun and educational experiences they can have with paper crafts, storytelling, drama, and puppetry. Randel McGee has belonged to the Guild of American Papercutters, the National Storytelling Network, and the International Ventriloquists' Association. He has been a regional director for the Puppeteers of America, Inc., and past president of UNIMA-USA, an international puppetry organization. He has been active in working with children and scouts in his community and church for many years. He and his wife live in California. They are the parents of five grown children who are all talented artists and performers.